WHEN THE W███████

A PLAY-IN-VERSE

Joshua Young

W9-AVT-159

Cara, has her bود up,
Kasey waiting just be you
she's the alley i ignore the
smell of oranges &
charcoal, i en listen
to the piano —

run —
Kasey has come to
claim!

THANK YOU

Josh

Copyright © 2012 by Joshua Young

Published by Gold Wake Press,
J. Michael Wahlgren

Cover design by Jordan Young

ISBN 10: 0983700117
ISBN 13: 978-0-9837001-1-1

No part of this book may be reproduced
except in brief quotations and in reviews
without permission from the publisher:

When The Wolves Quit: A Play-In-Verse
2012, Joshua Young

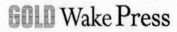 **GOLD** Wake Press

Boston, Ma

for Emily

WHEN THE WOLVES QUIT:
A PLAY-IN-VERSE

TABLE OF CONTENTS

CAST OF CHARACTERS & LOCATIONS

Major Characters:

The Preacher (#523)
The Guilty Boys
    The Quiet One (#521)
    The Guilty One (#522)
Kasey
The Sheriff
The Letter Writer
The Preacher's brother
The Congregation

Minor Characters (Selected):

The Deputies
The Letter Writer's Sisters
The Lovers (Deceased)
The Congregation
The Elders
The Elders' Daughters
The Girl Who Survived the Ghost Woods
The Captured Ones
Wolves
The Parade of Ghosts (AKA Bodies)
The Drunk
The Mayor
The City Sharks

The Names/Numbers on the List (Selected):

Kaveh Smith (# 17)
Dawn Smith (# 18)
Douglas McGuire (# 19)
Ruth Collins (# 20)
Emily Northrup (# 27)
Oliver Northrup (# 28)
Thomas Hansen (# 41)
Kathryn Hansen (# 42)
No Corresponding Name (# 58)

No Corresponding Name (# 59)
No Corresponding Name (# 147)
No Corresponding Name (# 148)
Bruce Powell (# 155)
Dicky Green (# 171)
Samantha Green (# 172)
Russell Lee

Gunshots

sometimes, at night, when the wolves quit.

there.

a gun's going off deep in the thicket, coming out of the canyon.

once it was two lovers who couldn't touch each other anymore. their parents
found them out the sunday prior—called them sinners, faggots, said things they
shouldn't've meant. so these two boys took from their fathers and walked
through the meat of town, into the woods, and down into the canyon. the air
wasn't warm, or cold, but thick and heavy. it smelled of topsoil and syrup. the
blonde one shot first, then took himself. no one knew till easter, and their
names were crossed off the list. by then the birds had got to them, nothing left
but un-edible.

another time, it was a hunter from the city
trying to find his way back
to the road.
he found a gray mass along the way,
but after the echo
cleared,
all he saw of it
was a thick chunk
of fur
and a few specks of blood.

tonight, the blasts come in pairs. they weren't too far away. if you listened, you
could hear
          whispers.

"should we?"
                    and

"no, he can bleed where he is."

there's a commotion coming from the church

this town is built on the vanishings.
it's part of everyone's story.

there's a list for each name—
it's tacked to the wall under the clock in the sheriff's office.

the preacher disappears.
no one notices till the church service sunday,
when the pews fill up,
and the sermon never comes.

from the pews,
a rumble of whispers begin sometime in the silence,
and rumors swell like a new bruise.

smiles creep up faces. some frown
and some keep their lips
and only listen to what gets said.

the preacher's brother took two elders
down the block to the preacher's house and came back
saying there was no answer at his door.
inside his bed is unmade
and there's probably a weeks worth of dust on things.

someone mentions the ghost woods.
that gets the congregation praying.

STAGE LIGHTS UP

dear sisters,

our town hasn't changed much since i've been in the eastern
cities. all the old places i used to go with you are still around—
that rope swing over the river, that sandy nook over the wash.

it's been months since we saw each other and i know i
promised to stay in touch, but after we said goodbye, i
followed the river out of the neighborhood, down to the tracks,
and headed north. it took a day to catch an open box car and i
rode that for a handful of days before ending up here. i didn't
plan on staying, but i was hungry and wandered into town. by
the time i got back to the rails, the train had left. i gave up
waiting after a day.

i found a room above the general store that's got a view of half
of town from the orchard to the gloomed woods at the edge of
town that i've heard people call the ghost woods. people say it
claims those who wander inside—gathers them up when they
breach the tree line.

ENTER STAGE RIGHT- THE PREACHER

yes, this town had a preacher,
young and tan in his day,
who used to preach of answers in arches,
answers in brick, in towers.

he'd spit sermons from the pulpit,
dressed in white
and black, weaving his hands
through the air in front of him
as if he was slapping the devil away.

some people said he took money from the offering plate
to fill his belly and pay his debts—

these city sharks kept moving,
finding him in the basements
of pubs, hugging barrels like the last
raft in water, in the alley
behind the station at midnight,
conversing with the lines of white
on the building, or at the grocery store's
window staring
in at the fake
cakes and fruit come mornings.

all this, typical for small town scandals and men
of god.

come august,
all that was left of him were slippers
and a bible,
and, of course, what part of him
he left in the wombs of the elders' daughters.

last anyone heard, the deputy
found his clothes out by the rails
cut all to hell.

one of the elders says,
they saw a red beast pulling him into the sand.
and one of the believers says,
the clouds parted and god brought him
home in a chariot of gold, salt, and fire.

but most followers eye the ghost
woods out at the edge of town and the sheriff
writes the preacher's name on the list,
because that's what happens when people vanish.

every night when people get to the talking,
the drunk says, one of the fathers put a couple
rounds in his belly and left him naked
at the bottom of the quarry
over near the fingertips of town.

❦

when the mayor wants answers,
real answers, the sheriff lifts
the preacher's name from the list
and all his deputies spread out
like an armful of geriatrics
with metal detectors, or the slow
creep of sickness through
a village. they round up the usual
suspects for questioning.
at the station, there are cut lips and bruises
swelling up under
eyes and accusations.

this is part of what gets said:

EXIT STAGE LEFT

when the guilty boys pass through the arbors
and valley rain,

it's like the dusting off of grandfather's
guns or the cutting
out of lover's tongues.
each flick of the wrist
howls at the slice
in family attics.

all of this, hardly
for convenience, but for something
tugging at the place below
their gut when the night gets heavy.

the old woman at the other side says,
"you young men should cover your tracks."

they had, though not in attics,
but the bottom of the quarry.

❊

that night, it wasn't them who drove out
and stripped off
their clothes, wiped blood from their hands
and faces and took turns
throwing what they could towards the center.

by morning, they were back
in their beds, and the sheriff had started
knocking on doors
for other reasons.

on the fifth front porch,
the middle daughter knows about trucks,
pissed off boys trying
to prove some points and talk of a plan.
she wouldn't give names,
but said she heard voices leaking
through the vents in the bathroom.

these ones never had reason to do what they did,
they took a life simply 'cause it was there
to take and they didn't like it…

the body isn't found for years,
when the troopers try to pull
a truck from the reservoir and find what they let plunge.

by then everyone's gone to wherever they went.

EXIT STAGE RIGHT

dear sisters,

this town is killing me with all its gray and rain sputter. keeps me up nights. i miss the punch clock misery from my twenties.

when the rain really gets going here, i miss the dust and heat of our high desert, and the way lightning stretched itself across the horizon in summer as if it had the need to tear itself into the clouds, and what rain came only changed the smell of the place.

here, there's a constant smell of bark and swamp water, and if i'm lucky, pine. though every now and again i smell oranges and charcoal leaking out of certain places.

there's constant misted-rain and everything's green, sprouting moss and ferns. on a map, this place is probably just a green square. and in the outskirts, everything is hills, slanting and rising, though this town is rectangular and boxed. when i walk through the cedar and pines, the moon gets massive, bloated, and lights most of town. it can't light the meadow behind the church, but when i walk it, the night lightens. though it's beautiful here, i'm craving the way the skyline looks with steel and glass at sunset.

the train whistles carry and echo from miles away into my window when it comes.

that's usually when the locals start locking their doors and windows, though i've seen no evidence of darker things.

OFFSTAGE – THE KILLING OF THOMAS HANSEN BY KATHRYN HANSEN

no. 41

no. 42

sometimes, stories can start like a coughful of smoke and the setting of a scene. in this one, three broken bones brought this to blood, and it started as she lied in bed tonguing the stitches her man put on her lips,

> when the night undressed itself, stark
> naked and waiting

for the slow leak of dawn and railroad clatter that comes early morning. she unsheaths the knife and waits for the first whistle. when it sounds, she cuts across his throat

> like drawing a line between two
> points on a map.

her boy keeps asking about his dad, the simple boyish kind of questions kids ask when they wait, but she doesn't tell him about the shallow grave under the house, covered in lime and a couple handfuls of cinnamon sticks. she simply looks

> her son in the eye, and says, "he's visiting a
> friend outta town."
> but his name makes the list.

it's not the smell that gives her up, but the bloody sheets her neighbor's mutt brings home on a sunday afternoon. a month later, the cops pull her son from her like boards from a fence.

> that's when something snaps.

when she's watching her son drive away in the back seat of a cop car. first it boils, then cuts loose and slides out. she shakes and jitters, and starts

growling at the topsoil and scratching
at the lawn.

the end of this story's got funeral processions and closed caskets, jail bars and a
boy who forgets all the bad things about his father,

all the good things about his mother.

so when the trial starts, he comes across town and fires his father's pistol
through the front window of the courtyard and got the bad end of a couple
bullets. when the smoke clears the bystanders

hear funeral jazz coming up from the rusted side of
town.

KATHRYN HANSEN'S DREAM SEQUENCE

at first, they thought it was the plague, said it was only
          a matter of time till
we were all bodies in a pile outside our own front doors.

but all i smell are oranges and charcoal. people stood on
          their porches for better views,
as if a crowd of eavesdroppers could cure just by listening or
          watching

the scenes unfold. but i flee, quick and quiet like a fox
          stealing apples from the prison
yard and they follow as voices usually do—

just marionettes gone free, shaking and rattling
          around upstairs whenever
a memory gets triggered or brought up.

these things are not things we lost in the fire,
          not the leftovers
of post-teen angst, or the hush of harbors at twilight.

                    this is heavy and sudden like catching an anchor in the
                    chest.

          ✿

                    is that laughter or coughing coming from the
                    tree line?

maybe it's just a coyote lurking in the brush 'cause here,
          secrets are damp,
caught in the space between the throat and the front teeth—

they only let 'em go when the time calls for it and someone

important is listening…

no, it's kasey, and she hasn't had a holiday in ages, years maybe.
          today she's waiting in hospitals, the burn ward
a thick smile sliding out from under her hood like a slit of sunlight

through a key hole as if she knows we will burn, and burn soon.

a train moans six blocks over and i'm hiding behind a stop sign,
          but something calls me inside—
something like an arpeggio in the key of d, dissected and put back
          together,

then fed back into itself—by the time the doors shut behind me,
          it's too   late.
i'm staring at her. as she takes me by the arm, she keeps saying,

                    "this is the undanced cadence of vanishing."

dear sisters,

this place feels as though it's breathing or whispering things about itself, and every day something new slips out from top window sills or out from half-open doors, and finds its way to me. last week, i started writing these down. there's quite a collection: the sound of the wind coming from the mill, the smell of maple syrup and pine after thunder showers, the way some places smell of oranges and charcoal, or even the way birds circle the courthouse in afternoons. yesterday, whimpers from some melody came crawling from the alley, it stuck with me all day, and while i couldn't quite place each note, i muttered its words. "when i learn to sing, it'll change the key of everything."

the biggest thing is what everyone calls the vanishings. people just disappear.

sometimes, i can see groups gathered outside the sheriff's office, watching through the window when he writes a new name.

here, people learn that the vanishings belong to the ghost woods.

past the downlands,
where everything tastes like salt
and limestone,
he touches the earth
as though it's the flesh of another's wife.
at contact,
hymns begin to swell in his head
and he can see the pews,
heads bowing,
and the preacher shouting,
"we are a hungry generation!"
this is where he finds the trail—
evidence of the flee.

he's not fond of the preacher, never was.
but he's a god-fearing man
and this search is his job.

it's the letter tacked to the list in his office
that sent him out. the writer had theories
about what happened to the preacher
and who was involved.

towns come and go, and he likes the way
landscapes tumble and roll.
up ahead,
footsteps carry like shouting voices.
the valley turns what noise makes
its way inside into heavy
swings of sound.

EXIT STAGE LEFT

the ghost woods first showed
themselves in autumn after
the first vanishing, when the
loggers started cutting their
way and found shallow
graves. the sheriff, then barely
two weeks in, came back with
the men to find only a wall of
trees, no graves, no work
done, and a pair of sandals
that belonged to the girl who
had vanished just days before.
it didn't smell of oranges and
charcoal—never has—but of
swamp water and wet cedar.
kids say, the trees uprooted
themselves, plucked the
bodies from the ground and
cleaned the scene. now,
people say all that's there are
walking skeletons and ghosts
with all their ghost hair
getting stuck in branches and
collected in holes, their ghost
voices howling like wolves,
breathing like rakes scraping
their way across the highway.

that afternoon, he went back
to his office and wrote her
name on a list. years later, he
would write GHOST
WOODS across the top—
not that he believed it, but the

town did, and he didn't want
to rule out anything. the list's
been keeping him busy,
unmarried, but never lonely.
he's got each name and each
life to keep him entertained—
he likes to imagine their lives
unfolding, picturing what led
them to the ghost woods.
though, nothing could explain
that type of wandering. and
as the names gather on paper,
on his wall, he can't imagine
scenarios, and this lack
wobbles around like a loose
tooth for years.

dear sisters,

for some reason, a parade of ghosts pass my bed after
midnight, after the wolves have howled, and the crickets have
forgotten what silence sounds like. they don't look at me or
stop or even haunt my place. they just walk through walls as if
they have places to be.

see, ghosts are quiet. no footsteps, no breathing, no voices, just
the sound of a piano ringing out—that sound before it quiets,
before a foot leaves the pedal. i slept through it for a week, just
chalking it up to house noises. but tonight, i smell oranges and
charcoal, and hear the sound again. i turn over, and there they
are marching through, eyes heavy, steps slacked and graceful.

at first, my skin turns cold and my body moves itself back
against the wall, hands rise like shields, fists in balls, but the
ghosts keep on, don't notice me.

they aren't transparent or white, but dusty gray and dull, more
like empty bodies coasting through walls.

i follow them.

once outside the house they separate. some go to houses, some
towards the trees, or the church, or shop attics. i watch them
through windows and over fences. they hover over sleeping
bodies, watching.

CUE MUSIC – THE CHORUS

he's at it again, singing his story
under the street lamp outside the courthouse,
pausing on the good parts, to slow,
to let sink and the chorus comes,

> "if i learn to sing, it'll change
> the key of everything."

though he's young with smooth
skin and well-kept clothes,
no marks of war
left on his body,
the smell of french cologne
and rosemary, it's no
secret that he is the town's
drunk, his inked fingers always zagging
through the air, conducting,
and what started
as maybe the follies of a young man
sewing oats and burning candles,
is now clearly a man on his last
leg, hacking and wheezing
between notes, and every couple
hours one of the deputies pulls up
to send him on his way.

it's just habit by now,
'cause he'll wander back
half-tuned and spilling
every detail he can dig
up from "the good part
of his story," his teens and early
twenties, before the coda—
those stories—

the kind other drunks
from the city and other
towns tell, when his hands
would find her silhouetted
curves in the window-light,
when the paychecks bought decorations
and evenings out, before
he had wandered from the station
to town and stayed,
when his body hadn't been peeled
oranges, stripped down.

he huddles and shakes like toothaches,
and no longer sings in colder seasons.
years back winter was his favorite time,
the air chipped at his throat
and he'd spout a melody,
sing himself through the snow
and rain, the melody
working men and women and children
brought home with them.
families became choirs ringing
out inside homes,

> "when i learn to sing, it'll change
> the key of everything."

before the preacher came with his tent
revivals, organ chords and acapella,
sermons, and salvation wrapped
up in the palm of his hands, these songs
meant something more than what they have become,
just fragments of words
and songs carved into the brick
wall of history by younger generations.

now this man is a fixture unkempt and dated,

and out of tune like loose strings on a fiddle,
just noise drowning out the sound of water
and birds and town-shuffle.

when the air smells of salt
and pine and the lower tides,
he's here, trying again, recalling
his past word by word,
humming that melody,
vibrato and pitch trembling what's left
when each quits, chewing at the mouth
of whatever bottle he can find, and going on,

"if i learned to sing, it would've changed
the key of everything.

MUSIC CRESCENDOS

though the preacher's trail
turned ether, all the names on the list
had trails.
some dead ends.
some end in the back of mills
or the overhangs of train stations
forty miles north, but some kept winding.

sometimes there are men, sometimes
women, but always a hasty grave,
shallow and half-covered in dried
ferns and strips of moss in the borders of town,
where the wolves roam when night drapes.

most bar-folk feel the itch to spit
rumors, but there are too many versions
stapling the walls. the sheriff
gets his leads because living in this town
taught him to filter.

today, he comes back with a woman
whose name made the list. she's glacial,
her lips unmoving, her eyes pointed.
when the deputies come to see her,
they ask the sheriff why the cell
smells of oranges and charcoal.

EXIT STAGE RIGHT

after the trigger-pulls, the guilty boys
didn't catch the train.
they took their father's truck and chased
the logging roads,
till they found the highway
tracing the bay.

see, their names were written
on the list two days before the preacher's.
though, that was their plan. the week before,
they filled the bar with boasting.
they would best the ghost woods.

on sunday night, they followed the preacher
out to the orchard.

now, in the next town,
small enough to learn and large enough to stay
unnoticed, they found a motel
tucked near the lungs of the town,
where visitors hardly went, and locals
found themselves on every sunday
when church was done and dinner waited.

at night, the boys drank in bars and read
headlines for news from home.

one stayed quiet and to himself,

the other made friends.
found his bed later and later, till morning would beat
him back to the motel, and the other
woke alone in the curtain-light.

STAGE LIGHTS UP

dear sisters,

i was on the bar stool, nursing a maker's mark when the voice
and the choral echo climbed in through the windows. the
"amen," the applause, the hollering, lifted me from my seat,
carried me through the doors, led by my chest, these sounds
tugging at my ribcage.

outside, i saw the glow from inside the church at the far
shoulder of town, heard a voice say, "we've been blessed by the
lord, we've been given a house of worship, a place to exalt that
is sturdy and made of brick and stone to keep our praises
safe..." the front doors opened and the congregation sang, "our
god is an awesome god," letting it filter into the street for the
non-believers to witness.

and i'm pulled right into that church and up to the alter,
coasting.

the preacher touched my forehead with his palm and it burned
though my body, turned my lower half to water. i tumbled
back, the spirit in me, shuffling around, scraping what it could
against my insides, down my throat into my lungs and belly,
and falling into my legs and feet, burrowing, pumping.

ENTER STAGE LEFT – THE SHERIFF QUESTIONS THE CITY SHARKS

in their warehouses of dank air and moisture,
and casinos popping with shuffling,
chatter, and tobacco smoke, they only
laugh when they hear about the preacher—
they collected weeks ago, maybe months.

they know of no other debts or city-trouble,
said the preacher's been absent since
paying up.

       ✶

empty-handed, he catches another trail
pushing down the coast and finds a woman,
number 58 on the list, her face
contracts when he stands in front of her.

she tries to turn, but he clutches
her arm and cuffs it to his,
says her name, and pulls her along.

she gives it up, lets it slack, and by mid-day
number 59's crossed out and the town-talk
quickens, but there's no trial.

he finds her body unmoving in the cell,
gray, barely warm.

EXIT STAGE LEFT

CUE BACKDROP – THE CHURCH GETS A NEW ELDER

on a sunday night, the train
came, heaving as it passed
through, stopping only to let a
man off. his body, thin and
fragile. he walked like an old
man, but breathed like a child
and smiled like a father.

the preacher met him on the
platform, brought him in, told
people this was his kid-
brother, though the preacher
looked younger, and they
looked nothing alike.

they ate in the kitchen,
turntable playing jazz,
conversations about things
followers would only wince
at.

the next sunday,
introductions were made and
he spoke.

"god has brought me here to
be with you. i was headed
south, when i felt a tugging at
my chest, it yanked and
yanked. so, i came west. i do
not know my reason for being
here, but i have faith that god
will show us together."

the congregation nodded as
they're supposed to, hands
folded, waiting for worship,
the prayer, the sermon.

dear sisters,

i know i spent all those sundays embarrassed of your theatrics,
of father's knack for making scenes when worship began. i
should've been used to it, but till i left, i was ashamed. you all
would flail, tumble through the aisle, spit tongues like curses,
and swear it was god's voice, swear that god's fire had found its
way into your limbs. and after service, dad was too exhausted
to eat.

i only started raising my hands to avoid judgement. not for
god, but for the churchgoers, and it became habit. but now,
god's fire is sifting in me, constanting boring deeper, constantly
speaking during service.

this is an apology. i'm sorry i thought it was an act.

OFFSTAGE – THE KILLING OF DICKY GREEN BY SAMANTHA GREEN

no. 171

no. 172

blindsided by her appearance at the diner's window, he looks from her glare to his eggs, watches them cool and waits for her to leave, but like always, her presence stays, clawing its nails into his side.

she starts tapping the window

when he doesn't look back, slow and steady quarter notes till he looks again, and she points with one handed jabs. she probably would've stayed for hours.

she likes to put fear in him. it makes her

stomach turn and her knees shake with pleasure, but one of the sheriff's deputies saw her there, heard the tapping, and left his place at the counter to send her along.

he doesn't know the details of how they met in the garden behind the church, both pulling weeds for money, or how the wedding in the church stayed small and quiet, and the preacher pronounced their names wrong, or the honeymoon in their own apartment above the grocery store. he knows the later stories, knows about the wounded walls in their old home like pock marks on a face, the bruises on bodies like water color spreading across paper, the screaming, the divorce, the scene in court with the bailiff and blood and "fucks."

he knows the poor boy just tries to keep his distance, but the she keeps finding him.

the deputy comes over and puts his hand on his shoulder, asks, "you ok?" he doesn't look up,

just shrugs the hand off and says, "no."

months later, when the town catches
whiffs of charcoal and oranges peeling
and some people say the ghost woods
are at work, these two names make the list and the ex
is gone, but the sheriff
finds her trail two towns over, headed
toward the eastern cities.

SAMANTHA GREEN'S DREAM SEQUENCE

there's a slick rumble lathering through my chest, and when it
    settles, the house is quiet.
the party broke hours ago, and all my friends left debris

in rows from room to room, so cleaning is easy. and as i gather
    the trash and bag it,
i catch the smell of oranges and charcoal lifting from the floor.

in the back room, the floor has been swept and cleaned, and all
    that's left is a girl in the shaded
corner of the room. she's staring out a big window and tapping
    a steady beat on the glass.

                i hear a piano ringing out from

behind her, notes lifting, as though her breaths have
    let them into the room.
i get real close, but can't see her eyes. i know she's here for me.
    the room seizes and buckles
when she looks at me and says, "can you hear that cadence?

it's yours. it belongs to you and what you've done. wait. listen."
    and she rises, but i do not watch her.

                the piano scales into the higher notes till it
                clicks out steady quarter-notes
                without tune.

ENTER STAGE RIGHT – THE BROTHER

the preacher's brother takes the reigns,
starts preaching when the followers
allow it—they need the word delivered.

his body moves differently, voice slower,
and his messages aren't the same.
he takes his time to make his points,
doesn't stomp the ground or slap at the air.

he simply speaks as though each word came from stone.

he points to ceiling
only when he says, "the lord."

he does not muster his sermons with fear.
he does not scream the devil's name, but whispers it,
says it slowly, so that they remember it as something
quiet and methodical.

✿

when asked about his brother, he does not
shed or crumble,
he only shakes his head
and tightens his lips.

"may the lord be with him."

during his first service, he tells stories,
one by one,
about kentucky and that old coming of age where
wheat is something you run your fingers
through, where magic hours
turn honest men to liars, where boys

cut their teeth on learning
what the bible says and what it meant to live by it.

the congregation applauds and believe he is speaking about
others.

EXIT STAGE RIGHT

dear sisters,

the church isn't fancy, but it's clean and worked in like a good
glove. even the pews have pockets from where followers-past
sat before they vanished or left. i've taken a spot in the back
where a young couple sat till early fall. they say their names—
and others—during prayer, so it goes long.

the congregation has come to know me not by name, but by
where i am during service. we are not a rowdy church, not like
back home. we always sing, and sometimes, we shout "amen"
or applaud, but the preacher's always going, always half-fire
and suffering in the heat of late mornings. his eyes never
resting, constantly flicking through all of us as he gives us our
bread and warnings.

OFFSTAGE – THE KILLING OF EMILY NORTHRUP BY OLIVER NORTHRUP

after the affair had run its course, the places they met grew heartbeats and singing voices. these places crooned, told him stories, and sometimes, they'd snicker at him when he passed on his way to work.

> those places carried secrets calling
> names and false shores.

every night, he let his pickup idle and he'd stare in through the windows of these places just to feel his gut turn and hear the wind play songs from ohio. when morning split out across buildings, he knew he was nothing more than a one-man

> carnival of mama's boys and glass jaws.

he tries and tries to let the guilt slip from him like cutting an anchor loose. he keeps saying, now that he's in her shadow, "cool it with the history."

> but night is a trap door in a bedroom.

the guilty ones—depending on their motives, how much time passed since the incident, or how long guilt is willing to trudge itself along and follow—usually end up trying to shake off nightmares from the night before.

> but some don't, some sleep like the
> dead from the southwest.

those are the ones who did not act in passion, the ones who hatched plans and followed through.

> they'll get what they get when the gates
> call their names.

the others, the ones with passion, can't always remember the dreams, 'cause they don't always stick, but the feeling does. it spreads, crawling from the skin, into the mouth, down the throat, to settle inside the stomach,

to burn, to wait.

this man, hid north of the lake in the east corner of the state—went straight there after he fired six bullets and left the house on market street. still, with all the quiet, the space, and the smell of pine and cedar, he can't find a night's sleep without the same dream.

these he remembers, though
they're not nightmares,

they're different, darker than dreams, warnings maybe, or prophecies, calling to him, telling him, something approaches for him.

it usually happens something like this:

OLIVER NORTHRUP'S DREAM SEQUENCE

in the window-light, i sit and wait for the undanced cadence
      of vanishing, for that thick
silence milking over my skin. growing every hour, my body
      collecting

              fat as if it was catching lint.

outside, the suffering moves and breathes, kicking up dust and spores smelling
of charcoal and oranges. trekking through town towards the pass in search of
better light, advanced medicine, and free plots

of land to make their own. passing through, we converse
      about those things
and the fires witnessed weeks back, when the counterfeiters
      from denton
congregated around the sewer drain outside the post office
      demanding something
real to crucify. we handed them a bag of love letters, but they did
      not read, they did not open
a single letter, or even hold it up to the sunlight, to steal a glance
      of its contents.
they formed a circle, heaved the bag, and set the burlap and paper
      to fire, singing,
"don't trust the suits they're all in cahoots with the evil one."
      and in the window-light,
i sit, still waiting, and the conversations have vanished
      with the suffering,
and now, kasey stands in the doorway with her hood up, like
      always, and she's nodding,
as she pours gasoline all over the walls, all over the floor, all over
      the man
in the window light, and she smiles as she strikes a match.

              this is how the room is set on fire.
              this is how it burns:

dear sisters,

have i told you about the ghost woods? i must have.

lately they've been slipping into sermons, and today, the
preacher went straight at it, saying, "they hold no mystery. you
believers know many from our flock, from our neighborhoods
who've disappeared among those branches. that's not mystery,
that's the devil's draw. unheard unless you really listen. so
listen to the sound of the devil's red mounth call like a hi-hat
through a verse. repent your sins and god will tune your ears
to know that putrid sound."

though i can see them from my window, i've never been, never
heard the call.

so tonight, i went to the edge of the ghost woods to cross the
threshold. i never saw ghosts breaching the tree line, but i
believed that this was their source. when i got to its reaches,
branches practically petting my face, i couldn't go on.
something tugged at the back of my ribcage, away from the
woods.

i sat on the half-standing wall of boulders and stared into the
depths. i heard things moving inside, just beyond sight, where
the dark curls into shapes and spaces. could've been ghosts, or
wolves hunting, or trees making plans.

then i heard the piano noise coming down from the mill.

a girl took the dare and, in august,
wandered in just to prove
that there were no ghosts
in the woods,
but once she breached
the tree line, dark came.
when she turned around her path was gone.

the trees had lifted
themselves from the ground
and thickened.
it was dark, but light
enough to see the skeletons,
shallow graves, scraps of clothing and human things
like parts of tents, rusted pots and pans and forks,
saddles, sleeves of clothing, all of this,
left in what could've been
a retreat or a scattering attempt to find a way out.

days after the girl went in, the trees
parted at night, let her
out into the orchard.
the sound of voices carried her
down the rows.
she heard them retreating,
gravel crunching,
and then she smelled blood.

EXIT STAGE LEFT

ENTER STAGE RIGHT – THERE'S BLOOD IN THE ORCHARD, BUT NO BODY

in the spider light of an orchard, a girl found dirt and blood in rows,
      bruised into the ground.
she moves to stay warm and alert among the shadows, shivers
      cause this dark cold
sticks to the body, gathers and tugs little flocks of night like cattle
      at the spark of winter.
and siren light clears the shadow back to where it came from,
      and all that color wakes her
from her stupor and shaking, to recall and retell what's been done.

LIGHTS FADE TO DARKNESS

SPOTLIGHT CENTER STAGE – THE SMELL

the smell has always been here, the town only thought it was coming from river
water and mud,

        but

when it started
pouring up
from the quarry,
from under houses,
some boys started
asking old
timers if it always
smelled like this.

        the answer spread

through the followers, then the town, pushing itself, squeezing through
open window
cracks, and slow shutting doors

when bodies showed, the smell thickened
and wandered through the meat of town, staging
itself in clothes, hovering above standing water,
and as bodies turned up, the smell began to settle
at the entrances of alleys and the backside of buildings.

        STAGE LIGHTS UP

each sister's belly held babies,
"bastards," the followers
called them
and so parents sent them
away,
forgot them. the followers
laughed
at these teenaged accusations,
at the lazy finger pointing to a
man of god.
these boys, these brothers,
they believed as brothers
should.

but here, it doesn't matter
what you believe,
what you know,

it only matters what is said
from the pulpit.

dear sisters,

i can't say i believe everything coming from the preacher's
mouth. some of it sounds too heavy and comes out sloppy,
spitting out of his mouth when he gets going for real, rambling
about god's love and sin's grip on man.

he does look convincing, sounds convincing, as if everything
that comes from him comes from god. he's never really behind
the pulpit for more than a second or two to grab the proper
reading of a verse or find his place in his sermon, instead he
likes to carry himself up and down the aisles, and in front of
the stage. one time he screamed, "god will protect you if you let
him! banish sin from your door, peel its grip from your body
parts!" and slammed the piano keys four times. its echo
hovered above the congregation for minutes before he spoke
again.

sometimes, he likes touching arms and shoulders and foreheads
if the moment calls for it. sometimes, he likes to sing certain
verses from song of solomon or leviticus in quarter notes and
he moves as though each part of his body are the gears inside
of clock, constantly pushing time forward, circling. i can feel
the spirit, even when i doubt. it burns in my throat, and my
ribcage tugs when he speaks. i shout things like "amen" and
"preach on brother."

it's clear the spirit's in others too, though they seem to believe
everything that's said. it's the way their eyes gloss over the
longer he speaks.

inside glows with all its candle and sky-light, the organs behind
the pulpit, next to the piano, and all the gold veining its way
through the heart of the ceiling, down into the cross against the
front wall. our voices rise and scale the brick walls and up to
the ceiling, coating before it quiets, and up comes the smell of

brick and copper, with the occasional hint of oranges and charcoal.

if i didn't know any better, i'd call it lust i see in the followers. they practically sweat it from their pores. they don't lick their lips or bat their eyelashes, but blush when he speaks, eyes watering when he comes close.

after church they speak to each other as though the other wasn't there, as though the sermon was spoken from the closet, inside a bedroom, at daybreak.

there are crimes and there are crimes of passion. if someone found
him right afterwards, he'd probably say

> it was neither, but a necessity born
> out of shame.

today, he'd tell you otherwise, and he tries to scrape it from his past
like bark from a tree, but it's tied to his ribcage and only tightens
when he tries to free it.

> the night it went down, he entered
> though the back

put a burlap bag over his head and stood over the bed—once theirs—and used
a pillow to muffle the shots.

> instead of shooting, he used the pillow
> to snuff her out.

took three hours of sitting inside his car, three blocks down, across the ball
park, loading and unloading shells into the chamber of his pistol. walking
through how it would go.

> when it was over, he remembered

how she'd lay herself on their living room floor, fold her arms across
her chest and say,

> "this is what i'd look like in a casket..."

> and

> "am i still pretty when i'm dead?"

people fall in love in the key of c and out of it with dissonance,

climbing its way into a scale.

that night, he made her bed, cleaned the house, and carried her
from the house to his car, and left her body a mile from the quarry
in the place kids call the ghost woods.

he tells bartenders about his dreams, the ones starting afterwards,
about kasey always clicking the chamber of his pistol and saying,

"what i do and what i should are like brothers."

✿

her name was number 20 on the list, today the sheriff's found parts of her body
under a stump. one of the deputies says, "who's that?" the sheriff straightens up
and pulls the list from his shirt pocket. he unfolds it and reads her name and
though he's never read it before.

sometimes, songs begin, almost like this:

RUSSELL LEE'S DREAM SEQUENCE

it's not a helicopter scaling its way down the side of the building
        this begins from train windows
watching willows lit by moon ricochet in the thick pitch—

someone says, "night hums when the moon's out," and sometimes
        if it's just right
you can see faces ghosted up in burlap, ready for robberies

they'll show at the edge of tracks, moving towards the wreck
        barrels slitting through
the damp mist of the hillside. now, from train windows i see kasey.

kasey and her black hood floating towards me, like a stalled truck
        through an intersection
as if the moon is guiding her. the train, even slower, and when i
        touch

my face, there's blood. only it's gray and thin as water.
        when the door swings up
kasey's there, smirking like a crowbar lodged underneath a
        deadbolt

                    someone says,

            "this cadence will be danced."

she's holding my shoulders, when the train stops at the bluff, its
        cliffs tumbling down
into where the pacific had laid itself. it's not salt i taste in the air

                    but skin, worse yet, the skin of my wife.

wolves howling sound like footsteps
in grass or leaves plucking themselves

from branches as if there's nothing else to do.

kasey says, "down there's where boys get covered
in dirt, boys become men overnight, they learn to earn
their keep for comebacks, second chances,
and the opening and closing of gates."

dear sisters,

i woke this sunday exiting the house. this is the work of the
spirit. i backslid into drinking and bended into the early
morning, but that morning, my body had lifted and dragged
me from bed, still drunk. i tried to retreat back into my covers,
but my ribcage became the needle of a compass pointing
toward the church, and my legs dragged through the alley and
out into the street, and through the front doors of the church,
into the my place in the pews.

ACT TWO – CURTAIN RISES REVEALING THE PLACE OF LIGHT AND SHADOW

a newcomer wakes in the place of light and shadow

SPOTLIGHT FOLLOWS THE ACTION

1.

history is kept this way

2.

i am not the only one here in this light and shadow

bodies stand in what light gets through to strengthen
their shadow.

word is, the stronger the shadow the better the chances
to visit above.

here, the sky is a river and many of us stand in place
looking up.

the air taste like oranges and charcoal, smells like wet fur
and wheat fields at magic hour.

the silence in here sounds like a grand piano
echoing in a hall.

expecting to wake at the bottom of the quarry, i became
speechless

there, watching all the bodies move around through
all the dark spots,

speaking to each other about how they got here,
starting with, "i woke…"

thing is, most of us know each other from town,
faces are all we get.

all that's left to do is catch up and clarify what went
down.

we know who put us here. most of us saw it happen.
the trigger, the knife, the blunt swing.

i saw two boys, followers, approaching the orchard's toes.
saw a couple sparks flare in the dark,

and felt a searing trail inside my chest. i went black before i could
see their faces, but i knew who they were.

3.

every town's got a place like this with all the bodies underneath. only some
ceilings aren't like ours.

some are made of rock or corn stalks, or sand, or ice. but it's the
same,
everyone likes to stare up at it.

this is kasey's place. but above, we believed this was the ghost
woods,
most of us here only make half of the list.

4.

could be months pass before i see her,

kasey.

only her hood's down, hair's up, and she's not smiling—tight-lipped
and head shaking as she approaches.

i ask if she's god.

"no and this ain't heaven—with all the lies you told up there, be glad i ain't.
you'd be kept out for sure, but our gates were always open for you. we were
waiting."

when she touches me, i understand that this could be worse,
that here is not hell, that here is not heaven, but here is my home.

5.

according to the rest of the bodies, kasey occupied everyone's
dreams,
but doesn't choose, selection breathes

on its own. i had heard others telling the same stories, what's she doing up
there, i couldn't tell you, but the big

body with the shadow thick as pitch says kasey's patrolling for the
guilty
ones, the ones who put us here.

everyone laughs at him, says we're the ones not in heaven, the ones
ghosting our families at night, that we're the guilty ones,

but the thick-shadowed body says he's seen them come in, seen
them
dragged into the far end of here,

where there's dust-light, past the older bodies. says, "we are the
victims." says, "there is a place for the guilty ones kasey's captured."

6.

we make fires out of water and watch it stream from the floor to our
ceiling. god how all we want is new bodies, real ones.

this is where i learn of all the visits.

we are allowed out together, single file, to rise at the center of town.
kasey does not watch us,

but i stay on path at first. there are no oranges and charcoal
when we're out.

that's how i know she's away, that's when i learn to stray.

7.

no one guards the door.

kasey's constantly mocking the ones with shadows like gauze,
craning her neck at the water above.

they don't stand a chance, but no one really tries to leave forever. we are
supposed to only leave for a few looks here and there.

it's as though kasey wants to see who has the guts to haunt in the
day. the one with the shadow

thick a pitch has a chance, but he won't go near the door before
night falls. he stares at the door.

watches for dark. when we're out, he wanders over to the diner and
stares in the window.

sometimes, he wanders around
behind the buildings.

i heard one got out, but returned probably days later, ashamed:
his family sent him away.

8.

days i stood under the light moving with it as needed.

now, i leave letters for my brother.

my shadow widens, darkens, but i don't dare leave when we're not allowed.

kasey's presence tends to be thicker near the door when the sun's still out.

it's humid and weighted, even when she's not seen for months.

i'm afraid to see her in town.

what she would do.

but when the rest of us line up, i keep wandering from the group.

9.

i don't believe the letters i leave ever get read,
but i know why.

to find them is a task itself. i leave these letters
on the backs

of stop signs, in bark, on the face of rocks,
on garage floors,

if people see this, they'll think some kids
are running wild, playing ghosts.

see, i cannot write in words, just the vertical lines.
the reader

must cross with horizontal lines to make
words.

i'm not sure if my brother's even noticed them, but
if he saw them,

i would like to think he'd know they're mine.

10.

so, we visit, watch our past pass us by, watch everyone age.

back down there, we talk of our visits.

sometimes, we gather at the foot of our old beds and watch
our wives and husbands or lovers with new men and women.

we envy not the act, jealous not of the sex, but of the bodies,
still alive.

we can never find the ones who put us here. most new bodies
start with that search,

but give up for visiting families.

a girl keeps talking about her killer, and one night she finds him,
sprawled in the river, gray.

she watches him, and by morning the current's carried him through
the canyon and into the quarry.

someone wonders why she's the only one who's
ever seen her killer.

the one with the shadow says, they've all been captured.

i am not interested in that kind of search.
what could be done anyway?

i haven't seen them once since i've been going up.

11.

someone opens their gray mouth, says, "these children will not know their fathers."

to some, it eats at their skin and softens their eyes.

to some, it quiets.

to some, it leads them to pockets of light, and though they thicken their shadows, they do not rise when it's not allowed.

their nerve doesn't have the salt for that.

12.

a new one falls from the ceiling, the man used to live down the
street from me, but i cannot say his name.

he wakes as though he was sleeping. he does not know who put
him here, but days later his son falls down,

holding the air like he's clenching a gun. he tells him who it was.

13.

14.

history is made differently above. or at least, the outcomes are different.

above history tells us the ghost woods claimed us, but we know
now that is just a bundle of trees with stories tacked to it.

one body asks kasey if she owns the ghost woods.

kasey laughs, says, "the ghost woods do what they need. they don't
belong to anyone."

every body that falls here, adds to its claim.

all of us have our names on the list in the sheriff's office—

so are the names of the ones who put us here.

15.

the wind comes, keeps cutting at our bodies, shakes us,
pushes against

our outsides like the weight of another, pressing down come
morning.

the wind comes when kasey's been gone for stretches.
that orange and charcoal

taste fills our mouths as though someone's shoved it through our
teeth.

when the wind settles, she appears, stalks though the center of us
without a word.

we wipe the taste the wind left on us, in us.

16.

talk of visits gets old,
and all we really do up there is watch.

it's clear my letters aren't being read.

we stand at bedsides, watching them stir in their sleep,
we stand in doorways, watching our children grow without us,
we stand at the tree line, watching our lovers love others,

      and it goes,

around the fire,

we share what we do up there around our families,
we elaborate, change our tone, wave our hands, clench our fists.

but the circle gets real tired of all that, of all that shame,
of all the if-i-could'ves and i-only-should'ves.

      conversation drifts

and the other bodies start talking
about the captured ones

curiosity sends me after answers, down past
where the oldest bodies huddle waiting
for their shadows to thin and peel away,

      piece by piece.

when i pass,
they don't bother to look up,
they just hum melodies to songs from orchestras

the place gets quiet,

sound leaves its place and dies as it lifts and shadows scatter
out and away from each other like fresh blood in water

i step through,
clearing them away with my hands,
and there, at the end of a tunnel

a hatch door.

i open it
counterclockwise till the door opens, swinging out
and inside, there are cells lining the wall,
and behind each bar there are human faces.

this is where she keeps the guilty ones.

CURTAIN FALLS

ACT THREE – CURTAIN RISES REVEALING THE TOWN AT DUSK

the sheriff's out and the town's getting used to the new preacher

SPOTLIGHT CENTER STAGE – THE SHERIFF'S MORNING MEETINGS

now, every morning he meets
his deputies at the back table in the diner,
where the late-nighters sip coffee,
smoke cigarettes, and slide
gossip back and forth across the table.

he wants updates, leads.

a few mornings ago, he assigned
each one trails, names to follow, and passed
out hand-written copies of the list,
half names, half xxs.

he said, "these are not vanishings anymore.
these are names of both
suspect and victim, disappearances and criminals."

the deputies don't eat breakfast at these meetings.
it's clear these young men let panic in to bump
around—

❁

when the ghost woods owned the cause,
fear took a breath.

murders taking claim, means safety's
been unhitched and reset,
and these deputies will walk home
tonight with loose shoulders and quickened eyes.

STAGE LIGHTS UP

dear sisters,

the spirit left me today.

came up from my feet, through my lungs, and out my throat. i did not exorcise the spirit. this was not a choice. it left when i saw the preacher climbing through an elder's daughter's window. curiosity sent me to the sill, where i saw his hands all over her skin, his clothes on the floor, his hips to hers like husbands and wives.

i see her brothers at the corner of the block looking over, waiting for him to exit. speaking to each other like wolves at the tree line.

to find railroad tracks, you
have to cut east through the
ankles of town and cross the
county line bridge, and even
then the train doesn't come
through more than twice a
month, bringing goods,
drifters, and passer-bys on
their way north.

standing on the platform, it
looks like all there is in these
parts is a station, trees, halves
of buildings and steady
rainfall kicking at the ground.

if the train comes through
when the night bleeds into
daylight as though it's leaking
through cloth, you can hear
wolves ending their prowl,
birds fading out, and frogs
singing in half notes.

the preacher once stood on
this same platform. but he
saw something prosperous in
the bleak skyline, felt
something tug at his ribcage
like a wire connected to the
sunrise.

could've been the smell of
oranges and charcoal that

pleased him, but whatever it
was, he had visions, saw a
congregation to feed, stacked
inside the brick of a building,
he felt the soft heat of candle
light and heard the organ
swell and voices gather and
spread in praise, and saw his
hands spreading fire with the
touch of god.

the north no longer called his
name, so he took his things
from the train and hiked into
where the town was huddled,
in the clearing a mile up from
the canyon.

he set up a tent twenty paces
from the general store and
every night
in the glow, he'd ask his
congregation, "you like jazz in
the city?" and no one would
answer, but some might
squirm or roll
shoulders, and he'd go on,
"jazz tucks the devil between
the scales and stops, fixes
things so you think what
you're hearin's got beauty in
it, truth in it, but all it's got is
hell-fire and adultery, bible-
burnin' and sloth. if you put
your ear up to a git-tar, you
can hear the chanting of hell,
'we got you where we want

you,' over and over, till you're
fallin' with the rest."

and they followed his words,
'cause he spoke like he meant
it, moved like a man who
knew how the world turned,
dancing his way through
sermons, spit-firing verses as
though it would be the last
breath he ever gave.

dear sisters,

last night, i heard gunshots in the orchard and hours later i
heard a girl scream. the sheriff's lights flashed till morning and
all the deputies scoured the rows, but all i've heard is that there
was a pool of blood, but no sign of a body.

ENTER STAGE RIGHT – THE SHERIFF KEEPS CROSSING OFF NAMES

the blame gets heavy against his back,
real lopsided and constant—
all those vanishings, all those names
let go to paper, when
they could've been the clear end of a trail.

he remembers who they were before
they were just names.

the deputies keep saying, "no one expected this,"
fear trickling out with each word.
he expected—or
the wiser parts of his young body once did,
but he kept blindly adding to the list,
pages and pages,
'cause that's what was done.

        ✿

first ten times were the hardest,

on porches, watching knees buckle and the way
parents and spouses grasp for bracing,
wailing those uncontrollable moans,
guttural, expanding.

he tells his deputies, "we're rewriting their lives."

this part of the whole thing is taxing.
it quiets him.
lets him sleep only a couple hours at a time,
and when he does, he dreams
about new murders, new

bodies surfacing—every lump in a field
becomes a grave, every stump
hides a body.

❉

one deputy returns with a man—
number 147—found
east, in a cabin between here and the next town.

that suspect won't give up
whereabouts, but he's got all of his girl's
things under his cot,
and she's number 148.
"i ain't saying shit," he says.
by five, he's all
black-eyed and loose-toothed,
spitting blood on the floor with even less to say.

a week later, the deputies find her body
in the husk of brush in the far corner of the meadow
behind the church.

❉

the sheriff knows this man and his girl,
saw them on several occasions in their lawn
battling out
jealousy and the wages of youthful engagements.

when morning meets the dark, he's still up,
watching the bruises swell and the sun
prying itself out over the trees.
the smell of oranges and charcoal
plows into the cell-room, and he coughs,
the citrus and coal scrambling into his nose
and throat.

the fit passes and he looks back to the man,
that body graying slowly.

he reports this to the mayor—
"every suspect grays during the night,
and now, i've witnessed it."—
the mayor puts his feet up and slurs,
"it's just the ghost woods coming to collect."

EXIT STAGE LEFT

dear sisters,

i've reclaimed my spot at the bar and the preacher's name
made the list.

pulling at my glass of maker's, i heard a conversation in the
corner of the room, where the light practically swayed from
dim to dark and back again, it crept over to me as if i was
supposed to be part of it, as though it kept tapping my
shoulder saying, "join."

someone said, "that's three more."

someone else said, "when was the last time there were three?"

"years ago."

there was storm that day. thunder smacking around like
someone's pounding the glass of a neighbor's house, but the
conversations carried in jitters and stopped only when the
storm dragged itself inside the doors, where men shook the
rain from their coats, from their hair.

the three they're talking about: the preacher, and two boys—
one of the elder's sons.

OFFSTAGE – KASEY'S IN THE DREAMS OF BRUCE POWELL

no. 155
kasey

i stop at the borders of dreams and peer in like a girl at a kitchen window, hoping for a glimpse of the life inside.

        but i am not here to look, i am here to collect

what needs collecting. a common misconception among the guilty ones is that these dreamscapes are mine. i don't paint these, or hollow out the rocks for buildings, or even hang lights in the basements. i just make use of them.

        and when there's a piano, i play it.

these dreamers follow me when i ask them to, and as i navigate, i can feel them tremble behind, following when they don't have to, complying 'cause they think all this is mine,

        or maybe it's guilt pulling them after me.

how i find them is easy, there's always an artifact of the crime—a weapon, evidence, a location—hanging around the scene, noticed or unnoticed among the actions,

        and so i find them in some kind of
        lighting that fits

the crime, and they look at me as though we've met, when we haven't, and say my name as though they know it, when they don't, and follow me, with no real questions,

        in to the edges of shadows.

there's no secret room carved in the back of a mountain, where i tell them their purpose. this is nothing more than me finding our way out.

and sometimes, exits sound like this:

BRUCE POWELL'S DREAM SEQUENCE

the sun quivers in the heat, but my arms bump and tighten.
        i hear a piano somewhere over the ridge,
down where the sun can't catch a thing, and the wind comes
        through the valley carrying

the sounds of wagon trains and children. my body whips and
        buckles like a scorpion tail at the end
of a fight. i tumble back against the brick part of town,
        where the farmland

gives up its arms, the streets still and moss covers where it can
        reach, and shiny things have not found
the way up towards the sky, they remain folded in the papers of architects.

                now, i can see her at the piano.

hood up, fingers poised, playing, then waiting, playing then waiting.

                she must sense me. she straightens up
                and lifts her foot from the pedal,
                and plays a series of minor chords,
                and when i'm close enough to touch her,
                she leans away

and starts playing a waltz, staccato and slow, but i think of winter
        and start shivering, i look at my feet,
at my bare feet, now covered in the water pouring from the top
        of the piano,

                and when i look up kasey's there,
                i can feel her breath on my skin,
                sticky, smelling of mandarin oranges
                and charcoal.

dear sisters,

i haven't seen the ghosts in a while, but now there are more
bodies, and there's one here who's got more of a face than i've
ever seen on these ghosts. its not just the flat mass of a head
like the others. it's got holes where the eyes should be and a slit
where the mouth is, vibrating as he parades through, and the
start of cheekbones, smoothing out.

i've started following this one.

this becomes a nightly task. i sleep early, just to get up when
they come. i'm still at it.

most of them just watch, but this new body never goes to the
same place. he's always marking things on the back of signs,
under seats, on the bottom of pews, on the corners of alley
walls. i can see the message at night, but they aren't words, just
rows of lines. in mornings they look like faded chalk.

OFFSTAGE – THE KILLING OF KAVEH SMITH BY DAWN SMITH AND DOUGLAS MCGUIRE

no. 17
no. 18
no. 19

anyone can smell its musk from the other room, somewhere between used linen
and dead skin.

hear it, too.

it screams.

sometimes, it sings in the darkest parts of morning before the birds start calling.

inside the room, bedside lamps keep half
of their faces hidden when they speak. one
touches the cuts under her eyes from accidents.

    "oh fuck, think of all the murder i could bleed for you."

but it's too late. the smell follows them to work,
the sound wraps itself around the fabric of their clothes,
each piece of hair. it wakes them up every two hours.

    "just this one time."

STAGE LIGHTS UP

THE SHERIFF'S DREAM SEQUENCE – THE GIRL

a gathering of followers surround the girl's body like a banquet
    of vultures on a hay
bale at noon. one by one they inch closer, and particles
    of rust and dirt

dance in the shaft of light pushing its way through the tree line,
    and when i
get closer to the backs of men and women around the body,

for some reason, i think of my father, or the way
my son strums d minors
on the porch after a day of plowing and pulling, crooning,

        "the night is still as if the night can
        forgive if it's warm and dark enough,
        but thing is, when there's blood in
        the air, the night does not forgive."

    ✿

i push my way to the center and crouch as though i'm standing on a
    patch of ice. her body is gray,
her eyes closed. i smell oranges and charcoal.

the crowd's gasps collect and spew out above them in one four part
    harmony,

        "the night is still as if the night can
        forgive if its warm and dark enough,
        but thing is, when there's blood in the
        air, the night does not forgive."

this does not remind me of my father or son.

        this is brutal and clear and has

capsized the hope of this girl's safe return.

CUE ALL LIGHTS

dear sisters,

some little girls and boys sing about the preacher. they made
up songs.

"the preacher's in a hole in the center of the ghost woods,
buried by the branches in the middle of the night. listen to his
voice it has sneaked up to the mill, listen to his sermons still
promising to heal."

i hear this song daily, lifting out from behind the school house,
from backyards.

i asked my boss about it. he said the foundation sunk and
cracked. all the wind pushes through that space—it's the way
they built the thing, all concrete and wood walls bending and
warping with water and age. he said it's been doing that since
he was a kid.

i've been up there when the wind hit, it came at me, swelling,
building speed, and turned the corner, coming through as a
choir crescendos through an opening door.

dear sisters,

i snuck into the sheriff's office last night and tacked a letter to
the top of the list. it's bigger than i thought. it's pages of names,
all tiny and hand-written. my letter wasn't a ton of proof. it
wasn't even anything more than giving them something i
witnessed right before the preacher died.

i'm not scared of the repercussions—they know i saw them. i
met eyes with the smaller one and he just stayed there, not
saying anything. it's been months since, but the girl who the
preacher took nightly, killed herself, and the after the funeral, i
saw the boys crouched outside the church, and watched them
follow him home, their bodies tracking in and out of the pitch,
breaths leading the way. at the preacher's house, they kept
quiet. the smaller one stood, face half-lit by the lamppost
outside the house, light and wide, his body bending into the
shadow. the bigger one didn't look at me, just huddled where
he was, rubbing his hands over each other in the pool of light.

i'll get to the point. last i saw, they were walking towards the
orchard, following the preacher. later, i heard the gunshots.

the mayor has the sheriff on the case and there's nothing to
chase. so, maybe this will give him something. if he puts things
together then good. if not, well, i did my part. but those boys
are gone and the last time anyone saw them was that night. it's
obvious what happened. people think they went out to the
ghost woods. they were talking about it all week. buying drinks
and talking. "we're gonna walk though the ghost woods," they
kept saying.

ENTER STAGE RIGHT – THE BROTHER'S ROOM

the preacher's brother never wakes
to see the preacher's body at his bedside,

never sees a message left on the backs
and bottoms of things,

only smells the orange and charcoal sifting
around his room in mornings.

this unknots him. and so he goes
to his bible and always reads the first
verse his eyes fall on.

he doesn't see his brother's
message on the back.

when he writes his sermon,
he thinks about his brother, about the way the spirit's

sensation never breached his body, how
he preached hoping to someday

feel that pulsating burn in his limbs.
but he feels something different

when he reads a good verse—
his eyes water and his voice deepens.

EXIT STAGE RIGHT

OFFSTAGE – THE QUIET BOY ATTEMPS TO AVOID KASEY

sidelined by guilt, he stays away from the bar light and jukebox twang, stalks the halls of the hotel, smoking cigarettes, 'cause he's afraid to see kasey again.

she comes around corners, up staircases, down elevator shafts like smoke from a barrel

claiming all she wants to do is talk.

he's managed to pull himself from sleep before the conversation propels itself forward. but last thursday, she came into the bar and sat next to him, said,

"all i want to do is speak to you..."

so, he's here, stalking, trying to remember if he knows her face from anywhere. but he can't place her.

of the two boys, he's the one who still feels.

he has memorized the feel of the pistol fisted and fired. wakes up sometimes, his hands curled around the phantom of its handle.

this tugs at the inside of his ribcage

✿

the one other one sleeps, eats, and talks

about how good it feels the know "the fucker's dead." two days later, he'll slide the paper across the diner table, and say, "so, we kind of made the front page."

the law found the murder weapon.

all the found bodies clear things up, piece by piece, shortening the
list, and derailing what started it. "doesn't matter anyway," he
says, chewing on a piece toast, "body's where no one can dig it up."

and rain curses the ground. its notes
sound like:

THE QUIET BOY'S DREAM SEQUENCE

when i slip and tumble into sleep, finally, at the week's end, kasey's
    there, waiting in the flicking light
of a derelict gymnasium. i smell oranges and charcoal. habit kicks
    and i turn to run, but she yells after me, says,

        "run and i'll find you anyway. it's what i do."

so, i swallow and turn back and cross the hardwood to where she
    stands, follow her out, through sheets
of rain warm as blood, thin as moth wings fluttering down,
    and into buildings of brick and ivy,
through hallways and sliding doors. she keeps saying,

        "not here, not here,"

till we reach a room, windowless and white. she turns, faces me
    and says,

        "when you wake, i'll be behind the tavern, waiting."

✿

i snap awake, my hair wet from rainfall, feet stiff from walking,
    and my brother's
fixing coffee, dressed in his underwear, whistling the melody to "ode to joy."
i sit up in bed and watch him move through the room,
    sipping coffee,
still whistling, not a speck of remorse coming from anywhere on his
    body,
his face is straight and solid like a piece of dirty glass, and in
    minutes,

        he's dressed and gone without a word.

his indifference to our crimes baffles
me. guilt hits
like anchor skidding across my chest.

kasey's where she said she'd be, puffing at a cigarette, picking at her nails. she sees him coming up the alley, regret slithering out from every crease of his face, anger boiling under his bones, building. knows it eats at him, tugs at his ribcage, kicks at his chest like an anchor cut free.

and he tries to act natural, to act as though to see someone from his dreams in front of him is an everyday thing.

✿

inside, they find the booth behind the pool tables, in the back corner, where smoke and jukebox twang drowns out whatever conversations need to happen. she's all blue eyes and smiles. when they sit she says,

> "you're good at keeping things hidden. i know, you've got things to say, and i know you got questions stacked a mile high, but i'm impressed with how calm you seem."

he can smell her and he remembers his dream. he nods, but doesn't speak.

> "first things first, kid. i'm not here for you, i'm here for your brother, the one skipping around town, drinking and picking up women, living off the money you took. him and me, we need to meet. i got words for him."

> "what am i to do?" he says. "i ain't his keeper?"

> "i need to know things about him. i need to know what will open him up? see, he won't let me into his dreams. i stand at the gates and watch him on trains, in banks, on dirt roads, at the helm of wooden boats, with women and men i don't know. i knock and knock on the gates, but he won't even look. he just sticks to what he's doing. i need to get his attention."

"i don't know what to tell you."

"i need you to tell me how to open his gates."

"how the fuck should i know?"

"what silences him?" she says, leaning forward. "what makes him so mad he can't even speak? that'll open him up good and wide."

and for some reason, maybe the way his neck tightens when he thinks of his brother or because to hear his brother's name sends him shivers, he says,

"talk about our sister. that's all you can do. guys like him are blocks of cement. won't even budge unless you go for the only thing he even breathes for. hell, take everything from him he'll be fine, but our sister. he loved that girl. talk about what happened to her."

"what happened to her?" she says like she doesn't know.

"they found her body at the bottom on the canyon," he says, leaning closer, so that he can taste her breath, like oranges and charcoal. "you know, down where they found those two queers. her and the baby inside, dead."

"oh," she says, pretending to put things together. "now...you did what i asked. what can i do for you?"

"you can leave me alone," he says, leaning away from her, his eyes watering from the smell. "i just want to sleep."

she just nods twice and sinks away from him, and he's alone, staring across the booth at nothing, the clatter of pool balls crackling and scattering over what the jukebox spits.

EXIT STAGE LEFT

dear sisters,

things have been bleak and the discoveries aren't really leading
to answers. the town's kind of on this middle ground between
closure and myth. every suspect the sheriff arrests ends up
dead in their cell. not murdered. just dead. i didn't want to
share this with you, but it's still happening. this morning a
woman. last night a man.

but on the other hand, morale has risen among the church-
goers. the new preacher has put their mind at ease. i don't hear
him shouting like the last preacher, but he looks serious when
he's at it. outside the bar, i listen to them pass after service,
talking about the sermon as if they were sharing it to someone
who missed it. when i went, we'd clam up and go to our rooms
to pray.

the preacher's brother
does not present the city as more than a place
filled with trails—
"god," he says, "is in all things,
even the putrid and dark."

he once lived in the eastern cities, knows what pools
in alleys, knows how filth grows where it's left free,
knows where sin nooses and waits.

"do not fear the city. it is not a beast,
it is not the arm of devil. sin can find us anywhere—
here or the city or out in the orchard.
our duty is to live as we should,
turning from sin, turning without fear."

✿

the preacher had things to say
about the cities, sometimes he's describe a monster,
shiny and concrete,
tied to the leash of the devil,
creeping closer, sprawling from its core
to choke the green and grain
from the earth, to consume
all the churches and their people.

he called buildings more than one floor,
"towers of babel,"
and paved roads, "the devil's path."
yeah, he'd jeer and seethe as he spoke of this,
cry if people went, and whimper out,
"careful followers, the city fishes for the loving,
disguises its lust for innocence."

⚹

the congregation nods when the preacher's brother
shares, and in town,
they speak of city-visits, but in the walls of their home the city
is still a monster,
and the preacher is still right.

EXIT STAGE LEFT

the business with the preacher has changed
the way the town looks at loss.
they mourn each body without judgment.
they hold funerals that stretch through town,
jazzy songs bursting from the line of people.

the list's been whittled and the sheriff's
still at it, never at these funerals,
never in town for more than a day.
his deputies too.

though, when's in town, he's not
found at the edge of the ghost woods
or at the blood spot in the orchard that still hasn't
washed away.

lately, he's been patrolling the quarry's
edge, staring down past that lip, into black that
carries
down. he's concerned about the smell
thickening since he brought the first suspect back.

the town's always had this smell, and he knows it,
but never this potent.

when he sees people, he says, "do you smell that?"

and in the cell room down the hall from his office,
bodies keep graying.

he can't place its source, but the town
keeps blaming the ghost woods.

he knows it's something else, something keeps

bringing him to the quarry—it tugs at his ribcage.

no answers surface, just new bodies to bury.

EXIT STAGE RIGHT

no. 522
kasey

my bodies would rise to watch. i would get over to the next town, and enter his room every night. but his sleep-schedule kept changing. i would find myself waiting for him when the sun rose. and till his friend gave me his key, i would just stare at him,

> or sometimes, i would follow him
> around the town.

but today, i enter his room and whisper about his sister into his ear. it tears at him and ajars his entrance, stirs his sleep. the border, once fogged and blackened out, starts clearing, more doors unlocking.

> there's something different with
> his dreams.

when he enters the dream he will smell the orange and charcoal, he will hear the piano across the way from a white room, in the attic of the town church, as the preacher delivers, like he always did, sermons.

✿

the guilty one enters through a doorway and i start playing.

> today, it sounds something like this:

THE GUILTY ONE'S DREAM SEQUENCE – THE CHURCH

i've only been in the church once, back when my mother found me
      out at the quarry throwing rocks at wounded birds,
but it wasn't the kind of church from the pictures, it was colder
      and louder.

so, she pulled me out quick and let her hands do the work she
      thought god might, and i'm here again
and the pews ring out like someone started pounding at random
      keys on a piano with fists,

and the floor's on fire, and the preacher's at the pulpit, only he's
      gray and dressed in suede the color of oceans,
he's screaming, "stay where you are. here: god has blessed,"
      then takes a breath like he's drinking water,
and goes, "his hands have ran its fingers through our grain,
      through our pine and fir needles, and sifted
our soil through his palms! look at our crops!" he trembles

                        and the pews sprout corn, tomatoes, and
                        lemon trees.

"out there, you will not prosper, the city is an animal read to eat!"
      behind the alter, the pulpit, the cross.
a stairway curls and curls, tightening like a fist, till my head

starts rubbing against the ceiling. i can hear a scale echoing up
      from the pews, octave to octave
and back down. at the top of the stairs, light filters through a
      pinhole, and i want

to see what's through it, so i kick and it ruptures open, and light
      crashes on me, only it's cold and licks at me
like a wave. i have to wipe it from my eyes with my sleeve,
      and through it, a woman sits on a piano

bench, in a room bright as a wedding gown, bare as fresh concrete.
　　　the scale stops when she lifts her hands
from the keys, and the echo fades. she slams her palms on the low
　　　end and the sound changes me.
i cower and the piano mutes. from across the room she tells me her
　　　name: kasey. i try to speak, can't,
and she says she's here to show me what guilt is, to teach me
　　　how to be a real man,
to give me what i deserve, and the piano swells

　　　　　　　　　　and floats and starts playing a progression,
　　　　　　　　　　tied to a candence i think i've heard before.

dear sisters,

the fog has lifted today, but from my window, i can see the ghost woods' shape in the gray mass. there are figures moving around, maybe wolves, maybe people, maybe the dead coming back to haunt us, waiting for the fog to reach the meat of town.

it's sunday and i can't hear the preacher's brother. he's too quiet, and the town's only gotten louder. in a hour, they'll leave the church, screaming about what was said.

yesterday, the church-folk found a body. the sheriff seemed distant, seemed hazy, as though he was somewhere else, when he crouched in front of her. this was the girl who claimed to have survived the ghost woods. she told people it wasn't that scary, that it was peaceful, and that she would've walked right through it, but there was a big concrete wall at the back with ropes dangling down from the darkness of higher branches. i never heard that story from her lips, but bar-talk did the job.

her name's never made the list. i saw her yesterday, walking through town.

SPOTLIGHT UPSTAGE RIGHT – THE MURDER WEAPON

the murder weapon gets discovered barrel up and half-rusted
in the swamp water
at the north end of the river.

this is where the drug smugglers from the south of mexico were busted
and carried off last november. they spoke in spanish, rattling off sentences,
kicking at the officers till they were shoved into their cell.

a junkie on her last leg
went to sink the needle's teeth into the black
sore hidden under shirt sleeves, down,
in the nook of her arm.
yeah, she found it before she could push off—
did it anyway.

      the sheriff had questions for her
      but she had no answers
      just shrugs and hand motions,

      he finds the trail anyway and waits
      with his deputies in the motel, three rooms down,
      loading bullets into their chambers.

this is how the boys' plans get shot to hell—

their visions of concrete stretching out as highways, into the arms of the
western states,
and golden gates parting, opening up to freedom and fame—
yanked back from their grips at four am, when the motel door flew open,
off its hinges.
bodies in black poured in, filled the room, waving their barrels.

one boy lies still and quiet, his body gray,
arms folded over his chest, just like the others.
kasey had come.

the other, simply sits up in bed, arms out, ready for the shackles.

STAGE LIGHTS UP

dear sisters,

i've been here a year. a year's long enough.

it may be a good while before i write again. after i send this, i'll find the first train, climb into an empty boxcar and take it north. in the city, i'll find myself a new job. i don't care what it is.

i'm leaving 'cause i can't take the unfolding of people and their families every time a body is found. last i heard, the list has been cut in half. there's a pressure in town. people looking at each other differently, as though all of these murders mean that the town isn't safe anymore. every suspect ends up dead. i heard that once they go to sleep in the cell, they won't wake. i didn't believe it, but for the last couple days, i've been watching the sheriff's office. i've watched the deputies carry out three bodies in the last four days.

and the smell.

it clears the bars on thursday nights, clears the street on saturdays so no one can smell what the shops are cooking. you'd practically have to shove your nose in a loaf of bread to smell it. it's gotten so bad that the followers make themselves nose plugs to wear during service.

the smell is the worst inside, thick as syrup and chalk in there as if there are piles of orange peels and lumps of charcoal filling the pews.

the worst part? people keep talking about the ghost woods.

EPILOGUE – THE CURTAIN RISES AND SPOTLIGHT FOLLOWS THE ACTION

there's a funeral procession coursing through the meat of town

the frenzy settles, but the sheriff and his deputies
are still at it,
the list filling with x after x.

the preacher gets his funeral.

there is no organ,
no piano, just followers
singing hymns between words, singing
hymns as they carry
the casket from the church to the graveyard.

the non-believers watch them from windows
and porches
and stoops, impressed by the spectacle.

by sundown, the hymns have settled into silence
and all that stands
left is the night's hum—crickets and canyon
echo, and the wolves tracking their prey.

the town has grown
tired of funerals,
both believers and non-believers.

and people say,
"the ghost woods wait."

LIGHTS DOWN

CURTAIN FALLS

THANK YOUS and HI-FIVES: J. Michael Wahlgren & Gold Wake Press; The Literary Journals that published pieces of this project (Alice Blue Review, The New Gnus, Weave Magazine, Breadcrumb Scabs, Used Furniture Review, Cut Bank); Richard Greenfield & Oliver de la Paz; All my professors; All my workshop folks at Western Washington University and New Mexico State University; Missy & Jessie; My son, Elliot, for being awesome; My wife, Emily, for EVERYTHING; And you for buying this book.

Joshua Young Lives in Chicago with his wife, their son, and their dog. For more information about his writings, films, and other projects visit, http://thestorythief.tumblr.com

CPSIA information can be obtained at www.ICGtesting.com
Printed in the USA
LVOW101328040412

276110LV00003B/25/P